Polyamory Coloring and Activity Book

By Tara Madison Avery,
Stephanie M. Sullivan M.S., LMFT,
and Jon Macy

Introduction

Interest in polyamory and ethical non-monogamy has spiked in recent years. As more people become aware of diverse ways to relate to one another, more books on the topic have been written, television shows have been more inclusive, and terms like "polyamory" and "ethical non-monogamy" have been Googled more frequently.

While polyamory has garnered attention in recent years, it is certainly not new. Even though the term "polyamory" was only coined in the 1990s, various types of non- monogamous relationships were happening long before that. From the swinging key parties of the 1970s to communal non-monogamous living in the mid-1800s, and the various non- monogamous relationships and kinship ties of the Comanche tribes, it's clear that polyamory and ethical non-monogamy have been around far longer than most people realize, or will even admit.

Therefore, this coloring and activity book is meant to be both fun and informative about historical polyamorous groups and figures, as well as current terms and information that polyamorous folks use in today's world. Polyamorous relationships can be both rewarding and difficult; especially for folks wanting to join in, it can feel almost impossible to navigate. Without guidance and information, these folks often can feel overwhelmed and confused. Polyamory is not just for those "in the know," - it is for anyone who wants to expand their romantic circle ethically and consensually.

This book is made up of pages created by polyamorous and polyamorous-affirmative artists, therapists, and polyamory experts. Many of our contributors have personal experience in polyamory. This book is meant to be a fun experience for you and/or your partner(s), friends, or anyone else who may find it interesting. It can also be a nice addition to an affirmative therapist's waiting room.

We hope you enjoy our coloring and activity book.

Polyamory Coloring and Activity Book
Edited by Tara Madison Avery, Stephanie M. Sullivan, and Jon Macy
Cover art by Jon Macy
Book design by Jon Macy and Tara Madison Avery
Stacked Deck Press logo by Gillian Cameron and Tara Madison Avery
Special thanks to Mike Kiefer

Stacked Deck Press
P.O. Box 922
Dana Point, CA 92629
https://www.stackeddeckpress.com

ISBN (paperback): 979-8-9883992-0-9
SDP00019

SDP ♥ STACKED DECK PRESS

Benny Hollman

The Bloomsbury Group

Tara Madison Avery

Are You Polyamorous?
Take this Quiz and Find Out!

Sandy Peace, PsyD

Read each question and circle the answer that most closely matches how you feel and think.

1. Do you like leftovers?
    1. I make a big pot of food on Sunday and eat it the whole week.
    2. I have a consistent schedule of meals that I rotate weekly. Today is meatloaf day.
    3. If it's really good, I'll happily eat it a few times! Mostly I eat leftovers to not waste food or because it's convenient.
    4. I get bored eating the same dish twice. Variety is the spice of life!

2. How do you deal with conflict?
    1. I don't have conflict - I always get my way. Or, conversely, I always let others get their way.
    2. I don't like conflict and avoid it at all costs. It'll resolve itself with time.
    3. I speak up when I really need to, but most of the time I let it ride. You have to pick your battles.
    4. I voice my needs, listen to others' needs, and try to find a win/win solution. My motto is: "Everyone's needs get met. All desires will be considered and negotiated."

3. How do you feel about routine?
    1. I hate not having a routine and get anxious when things don't go as planned.
    2. I have a daily routine I like to stick to, but can change my plans with advance warning.
    3. I have a daily routine, but I also do things spontaneously or change plans spur of the moment.
    4. Routine is boring! I prioritize self-care and effectiveness, but I like to mix it up.

4. Do you consider yourself a complex person?
    1. I am a simple person with simple needs. Why waste time thinking too much?
    2. I have a few things that I'm really into, but I don't have an interest in trying new things. I've got myself pretty much figured out... no need to dig deeper.

3. I have been to therapy, am introspective, and value self-growth. I've found a good balance in my life, but I challenge myself to try new things. It's good to stretch your comfort zone.
4. There are so many aspects to me that I will never know them all even if I spend my whole life looking. My life orientation is to learn as much about myself as possible and have meaningful experiences and interactions to help me grow.

5. Are you looking for or have you found "The One"?
    1. YES! I want that one person who will be my best friend, lover, and life companion. It's possible!
    2. Yes. I have (or want to have) my soul mate. I have friends that I spend time with, but most of my free time is spent with my partner.
    3. Yes, but I'm beginning to wonder if this is really possible. I am sometimes attracted to other people and wonder what it would be like to have an intimate/romantic/sexual connection with them as well as my partner.
    4. The "one true love" is an imaginary construct. No one can meet all my needs and I don't want to be responsible for meeting someone else's every need. I have friends, lovers, family, a career, etc. that all help satisfy my needs. I believe it's possible to have many soul mates in my lifetime.

Benny Hollman

6. Are you bisexual or pansexual?
    1. Hell no! Bisexuality doesn't really exist. Pick a side, people. And WTF is pansexual? You're just making up words.
    2. No. I don't really get it, but I'm accepting of those who are.
    3. Yes. And it sometimes makes me sad that I won't be able to express the full range of my sexuality with one partner.
    4. Yes! And I'm taking full advantage of all the juicy benefits.

7. Do you need community?
    1. I'm a lone wolf (if single). My partner is all I need to be happy (if partnered).
    2. I'm close with my family, but don't have many outside friends.
    3. I rely on family and friends for a sense of community.
    4. I built my own tribe.

8. How do you deal with the breakup of a long-term or serious relationship?
    1. Breaking up is not an option. Once you've committed to someone, you need to stick together no matter what.
    2. I'm devastated and do everything I can to get back together and make it work. The breakup often lasts several months - we still talk regularly and have sex even though we're not together.
    3. It makes me sad, and I realize that sometimes things don't work out. I spend some time grieving (sometimes a long time), but I get back out there and look for love or find contentment being single.
    4. I'm sad and I know that breakups are just part of being in love. People change and grow, so there is no use trying to save a connection that is no longer there. I'm thankful for every minute we had together and see if a friendship is still possible. I shake the blues by spending time with other friends and lovers.

9. How do you define a committed, serious relationship?
    1. When you say "I do" that's it. You're together forever, no matter what. Even if you're not in love anymore. Even if the other person is not sexually faithful. Marriage is sacred.
    2. When you get married, it's with the intention of a lifetime commitment. When challenges arise you work it out, forgive and forget, or just ignore them. Divorce is an option for people if they can't work out their problems... or if someone better comes along.
    3. When you move in together, that's commitment. If we break up, it might hurt, but it doesn't need to be messy. Marriage is not necessary, but it might happen at some point if living together works out – or if one of us needs to get on the other person's health insurance.

4. I'm committed to love, friendship, sex, maybe even living together or marriage as long as it works for both of us. People change and relationships change. If it's not working, we change our expectations and level of commitment. We might even stay best friends. Who knows... we might be lovers again in a few years.

10. Have you ever cheated on your partner?
    1. No. That is a sin.
    2. Not even at Monopoly. I've thought about it, then felt guilty as hell.
    3. Yes, but I'm not proud of it. OR No, but I've gotten close a few times.(Kissing someone while drunk or sexting with an ex doesn't count as cheating, does it?)
    4. No. I only have sex with other people with my partners' knowledge and consent. Cheating is morally wrong – it takes away your partner's agency. I believe in consensual non-monogamy that is negotiated between all parties involved. If I break an agreement or boundary we have about sex, that is cheating. If I do break an agreement I fess up and we talk about it.

11. How do you feel about sexual infidelity?
    1. It's morally wrong. Sexual fidelity is the bedrock of our society – it's what separates us from animals. People who cheat are heartless.
    2. I think it's wrong. From time to time I see an attractive person and fantasize about having sex with them, but I immediately feel guilty. (One time I did cheat and it resulted in a break up.)

Benny Hollman

3. Sometimes it's right and sometimes it's wrong. If you are married to someone you're not having sex with I think it's only natural to have sex with other people. We can't be expected to be celibate the rest of our lives just because we're in a (sexless) monogamous relationship. What they don't know won't hurt them.
4. Is this a trick question? Having sex with other people with the knowledge and consent of everyone involved is totally ok. Going behind someone's back and having sex with someone else is wrong, but having sex with multiple people is natural. The Bonobos have it right!

12. Do you look at people other than your partner and find them attractive?
    1. No. That is totally disrespectful of my partner.
    2. Yes. But I do it on the sly so my partner doesn't see me.
    3. Yes. It's only natural. Sometimes I even tell my partner.
    4. Yes. There is so much beauty in the world to soak up. I'm open with my partner about my attractions. They accept this and sometimes it turns them on to hear about it.

13. Do you like to dress up in costumes?
    1. No way. That is for kids. I'm an adult.
    2. I sometimes do for a party (i.e. Halloween, Masquerade Ball) where others are dressed up.
    3. Yes! I love going to parties or out on the town in costume and do so whenever the opportunity presents itself.
    4. Yes! I love expressing different parts of my personality through costumes. I don't need an excuse to wear a costume. I do it when the desire moves me.

14. Do you read/watch sci-fi or fantasy?
    1. No. That stuff is too nerdy for me.
    2. I've read/watched some of the classics, but not on a regular basis.
    3. Yes. They are some of my preferred genres. I'd consider myself a sci-fi/fantasy geek.
    4. I speak Klingon, Jawa, and Elvish.

15. Are you religious?
    1. Yes. I'm a by-the-book believer.
    2. Yes. I grew up religious and continue to practice. My faith is pretty open and accepting of other beliefs, but this is the one for me.
    3. I grew up religious but converted to a more liberal/earth-based/spirituality as an adult.
    4. I'm not into organized religion, but I believe in love and human connection. I consider myself spiritual (but not religious), humanist, agnostic, or atheist.

16. How do you feel about change?
    1. I hate change! I avoid it at all costs.
    2. Change is inevitable, but it sucks.
    3. Change is inevitable, so I roll with it.
    4. Change is good!

17. Do you like to talk about your emotions?
    1. Emotions? I don't get emotional, and if I do I try not to think about it.
    2. I have emotions, but I don't share them with others.
    3. I am aware of my emotions, and I talk about them with trusted others when needed.
    4. I live for processing emotions!

18. Have you ever fallen in love with two people at the same time?
    1. Absolutely not. Once someone has my heart, I'm all theirs.
    2. Yes, but I would never tell my partner and immediately dismiss the thought.
    3. Yes, and I dated them both, but they didn't know.
    4. Yes, and I'm dating both of them. In fact, we're all having dinner together now.

19. What does the acronym AFGE mean to you?
    1. American Federation of Government Employees.
    2. Animal and Flower Growing Experts.
    3. Atheists For Government Eradication.
    4. Another Fucking Growth Experience.

20. What is NRE?
    1. Nelson Racing Engines
    2. Non-Recurring Engineering
    3. Natural Resources and Environment
    4. New Relationship Energy

21. Have you ever fantasized about having sex with someone other than your partner? Or with more than one person at the same time?
    1. Sexual fantasies are a form of cheating on your partner. I don't let my mind go there.
    2. Sometimes, but I feel guilty about it so I stop myself. And I certainly don't tell my partner!
    3. Of course. Everyone does. I've even told my partner about a couple of fantasies I've had.
    4. I live the dream! My fantasies are my reality.

22. Do you flirt with people other than your partner?
    1. No. Flirting is the same as cheating. It's disrespectful to my partner and misleading to the person I'm interacting with.
    2. Sure. When I'm out on the town with friends I flirt, but never in front of my partner. It's fun, but I usually feel guilty the next day.
    3. Yes, but usually only when I'm at a party or a bit tipsy. My partner teases me for being a shameless flirt. It even brings a little spice to our relationship.
    4. Yes. I love exchanging flirty energy with other people. It's such a life-affirming, connecting activity. My partner(s) told me they love to see me strut my stuff and make other people feel good. I feel energized by these interactions and my partner(s) benefit from this energy. Compersion is real.

23. Do you think it's possible to love more than one person at a time?
    1. No. If I love someone other than my partner it takes away from the love I have for them.
    2. Love is reserved for my spouse, children, and family members.
    3. Of course. I love my partner, kids, family, and friends. I have a general sense of love for the world.
    4. Absolutely! Love is abundant and I want to be a force of love in the world.

Benny Hollman

24. When you're dating multiple people, do you let everyone know?
    1. I only date one person at a time. After the first date we are together monogamously, and once we have sex that means we are committed to each other.
    2. I date multiple people but only until I have had at least 3-4 dates with one person; I don't share that I'm dating others but will tell them I am exclusively seeing them after the third or fourth date. I don't have sex until I know we are exclusive.
    3. I date multiple people and will talk about my sexual history, but I don't disclose I'm having sex with other people at the same time.
    4. I let new dates know up front that I see multiple people and have other sexual partners. I do not share specifics for the privacy of my other partners unless they are open it, then I will share details.

25. Do you get jealous when your partner flirts with someone else?
    1. What!?! Someone's flirting with my partner. I'm gonna kick their ass!
    2. Of course! If you get jealous, that's how you know you really like someone.
    3. I used to get jealous, and sometimes I still do, but I know how to manage it.
    4. It's pretty sexy to see the flirty energy between my partner and someone else. Sure, I'm only human and I do experience jealousy sometimes, but I know it's only an emotion and I don't have to act on it. I often get a sense of compersion when I see my partner enjoying interacting with other people in a flirty way.

Benny Hollman

To tally up, give yourself 1 point for every answer number 1 you've chosen, 2 points for every answer number 2, 3 points for every answer number 3, and 4 points for every answer number 4. Find your total below.

25-39 Definitely NOT Polyamorous. Your first response is, "Polyamory is just a fancy word for cheating. It's one man and one woman. Period." If you're gay, you stick to the traditional notion of monogamous partnership and marriage. You believe in the happily ever after fairy tale and are looking for, or have found, "The One."

40-62 Probably Not Polyamorous. Your first response is, "I could never do that. One partner is enough," but you are open to the idea that it is an option that works for some. Your main style of relating may be "serial monogamy" and your love is focused on your partner and close family.

63-84 Considering Polyamory. Your first response when you heard of polyamory was, "Is that allowed?" Your second response was, "How do you get an awesome life like that?" Your third response was to read The Ethical Slut and join a polyamory forum online. The idea of loving abundantly makes you happy and full of energy. Go ahead – fuck around and find out (with the knowledge and consent of everyone involved)!

85-100 Definitely Polyamorous. Why are you even taking this test? You know you are polyamorous! If you're not already acting on this knowledge, you will soon. You have the disposition, self-knowledge, communication skills, and maturity to balance loving multiple people and to problem solve the inevitable relationship challenges. So get out there and love some people already!

Egon Mouth

14

Communes of Polyamorous History

Kerista

Kerista was originally founded by John "Bro Jud" Presmont in New York city in 1956. It began as a group of loosely connected utopian communities with presences in New York, Los Angeles, and San Francisco, but the San Francisco commune would become its center in the 1970s and 80s. Members of Kerista followed many of the principles of the hippy movement and practiced a form of non-hierarchical non-monogamy they called polyfidelity. While Kerista aspired to egalitarianism, the charismatic Bro Jud often dominated decision making.

Lucy Allen

WORD SEARCH

```
N  S  B  Y  R  W  I  A  R  C  O  W  G  I  R  L  T  F  A  H  D
Z  D  L  J  P  E  M  B  Q  N  O  F  C  B  D  N  E  X  W  I  S
O  T  E  V  K  Y  E  I  H  L  G  M  E  T  U  E  K  M  B  E  U
H  D  X  E  S  I  U  P  A  J  Z  I  P  F  C  A  L  H  S  R  W
C  N  M  E  T  A  M  O  U  R  C  H  E  E  Q  F  O  T  Y  A  R
P  F  A  G  N  V  C  L  Y  X  P  O  T  Y  R  M  W  O  A  R  J
O  H  K  S  Y  R  G  Y  I  Z  S  G  A  F  E  S  O  M  N  C  G
L  N  P  F  E  D  Z  U  Y  D  U  R  M  B  X  K  I  R  V  H  Y
Y  Q  O  L  P  C  O  M  E  T  N  J  O  L  A  M  E  O  D  Y  R
K  F  L  T  D  V  R  S  Q  C  I  F  U  B  L  E  G  P  N  H  A
O  D  Y  F  R  K  W  O  U  K  C  L  R  F  R  O  Y  P  D  E  M
I  E  C  Z  O  I  J  R  F  G  O  A  E  O  K  B  Q  H  V  X  I
T  W  U  X  N  S  A  U  N  O  R  G  T  D  C  I  K  T  W  S  R
Y  A  L  G  J  U  C  D  S  X  N  A  Z  P  I  R  H  M  Q  N  P
X  S  E  Q  O  C  H  U  Y  T  L  P  S  Y  U  F  T  H  Y  M  N
E  R  U  W  L  R  I  G  X  A  O  Q  V  O  H  B  Y  I  L  R  E
P  T  M  N  B  U  N  R  C  E  R  J  M  E  G  I  D  L  L  K  H
O  V  G  R  D  A  G  S  W  F  X  A  P  W  Y  O  B  W  O  C  T
H  Y  S  E  T  F  E  H  L  C  R  G  O  R  V  T  Z  K  W  P  C
Z  U  A  G  W  Q  P  E  D  A  U  Q  I  F  M  D  B  T  S  L  H
R  A  G  A  M  Y  Z  X  P  A  R  A  D  O  U  R  I  N  E  G  R
```

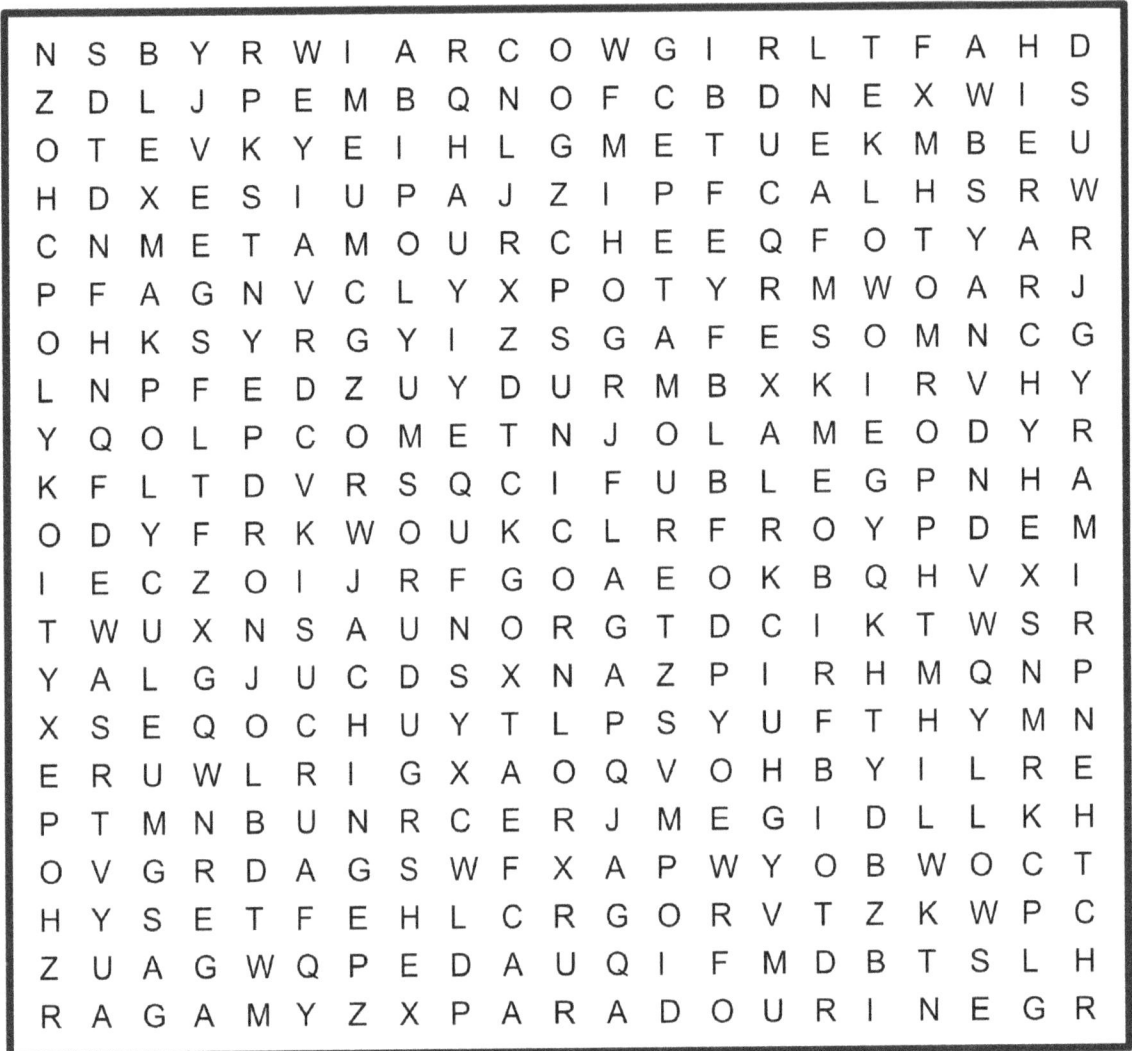

AGAMY	ESCALATOR	PETAMOUR	SWOLLY
BIPOLY	HIERARCHY	POLYCULE	TRIAD
COMET	HINGE	POLYKOITY	UNICORN
COMPERSION	METAMOUR	POLYFIDELITY	VEE
COWBOY	NRE	PRIMARY	VETO
COWGIRL	OPP	QUAD	
DELTA	PARAMOUR	SWINGER	

Samantha Johnston
Solution on page 48.

Communes & Polyamorous History

Lavender Hill

The Lavender Hill commune was a gay and lesbian liberationist intentional community formed in Ithaca, New York in the 1970s. Its members lived and loved communally, often participating in group sex and "love fests" as well as playful gender transgression. Member Larry Mitchell wrote the fairytale manifesto The Faggots & Their Friends Between Revolutions based in part on his experience living at Lavender Hill, and fellow member Ned Asta illustrated the book.

Lucy Allen

Carrie Metz-Caporusso

SCRAMBLE

Unscramble the Poly Terms and the Five Love Languages

IRENICEGV SGFTI

MAOLYOYPR

YHCPISAL HTUOC

CMOSPNIOER

CAST FO RCSEVIE

ESUYCORELP

ROWDS FO FAIAORINMFT

LLEPUYOC

QAUYTLI TEIM

TAMMOUER

Find the solutions on page 49

Samantha Johnston

Sonya Saturday

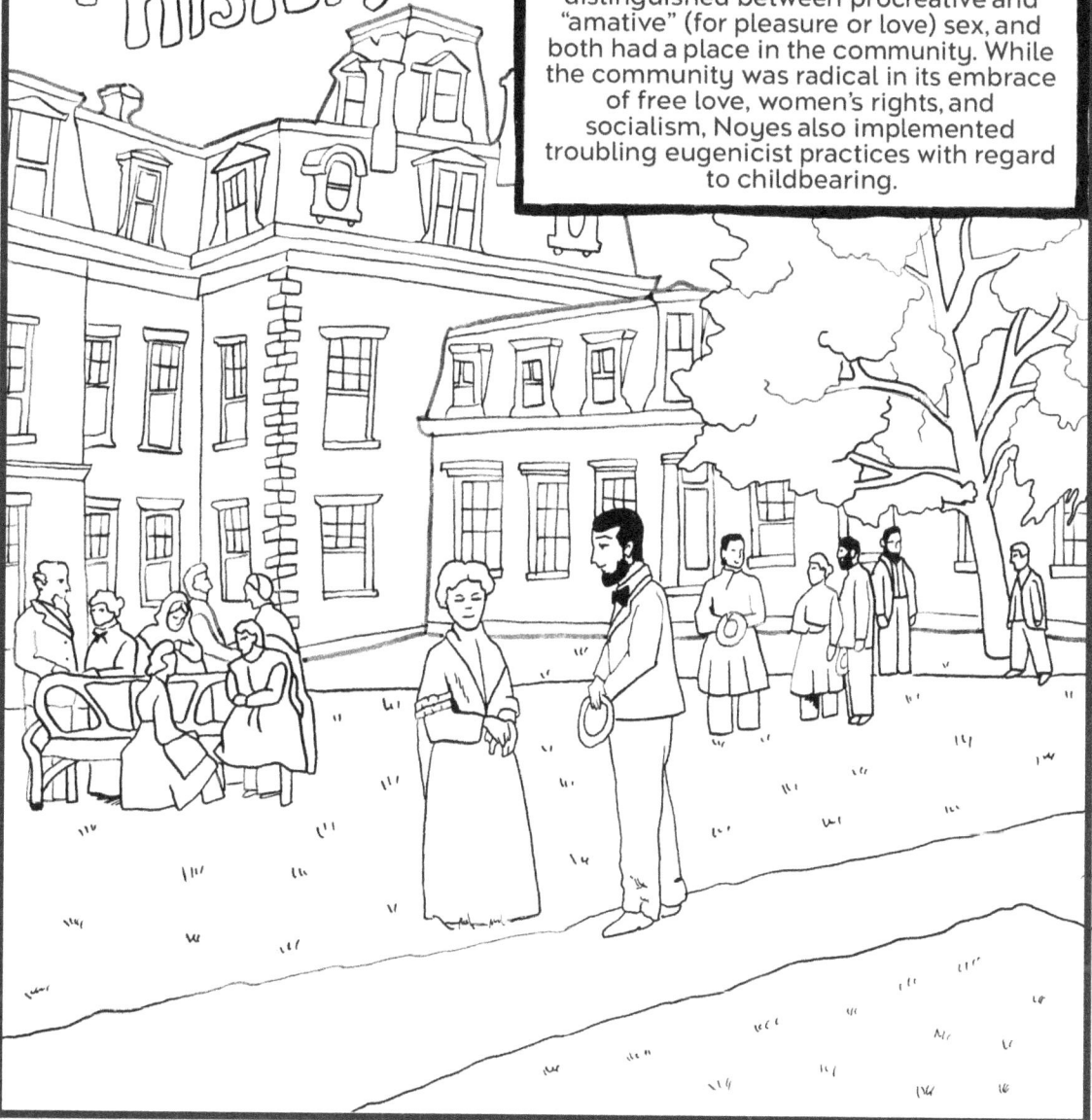

Communes of Polyamorous History

The Oneida Community

Founded in 1848 by utopian preacher John Humphrey Noyes, the Oneida Community was a religious commune in upstate New York. The community practiced group marriage and communal ownership of property. Noyes distinguished between procreative and "amative" (for pleasure or love) sex, and both had a place in the community. While the community was radical in its embrace of free love, women's rights, and socialism, Noyes also implemented troubling eugenicist practices with regard to childbearing.

Lucy Allen

Tara Madison Avery

R.A.D.A.R.

Multiamory's Monthly Relationship Check-In

1 REVIEW

Review what happened in your lives during the past month. No discussion yet, just facts. If you've had a R.A.DA.R. before, discuss your past action points.

2 AGREE THE AGENDA

Make a list of what you'll discuss. In addition, we recommend including the set topics below in your agenda, *even if there isn't anything "wrong."*

Quality Time - Sex - Health - Other Partners (if non-monogamous) **Fights/Arguments - Money - Work/Projects - Travel - Family - Household**

3 DISCUSS

Go through the agenda with your partner. A lot of different emotions may come up, and that's okay! Use compassion, empathy, and active listening. If things get heated, it's okay to take a break and cool off before coming back to it.

4 ACTION POINTS

As you discuss and resolve problems, come up with tangible, achievable action points to ensure you're both taking steps to grow and improve. You can always check on progress and change action points that aren't serving you at your next R.A.D.A.R.

5 RECONNECT

You made it through! End on a positive note by reconnecting to your partner. Verbally appreciate and compliment each other, give affectionate touch, or share a fun activity you both enjoy.

MULTIAMORY

©Multiamory, LLC   Visit Multiamory.com for more

Multiamory and Gillian Cameron

23

Puzzling Out Polyamory

by Janet W. Hardy

Across

1 Neopagan commitment ceremony which may include jumping over a broom
9 Exist
10 Brownish green
12 Frozen water
14 Roughly a thirtieth of a *mes*
16 Hither's partner
17 One man, one woman and some kids, all under one roof
18 Barbara __, progressive Representative from Oakland, CA
19 Statistical mean (abbr)
21 Niles's and Velma's lust object
24 Between your thigh and your shin
25 People who may not approve of your relationship (unless you're very lucky)
27 First a princess, then a general
29 A way to get to the air terminal when none of your lovers can drive you
34 An event where your polycule might like to meet up
35 Prefix meaning "both"
37 Belief in a deity
38 Sound heard on Old McDonald's commune
40 Crying Game costar
42 Vita __, half of a well-known cross-orientation relationship
47 Black sticky stuff
48 What you might like to exchange with your lovers when they're not around
49 Right here in Paris
50 A lovely way to greet your Hawaiian lovers
51 Sometimes we wish we had one of these to find our way around poly
52 A relationship style much more common in nature than sexual monogamy

Down

1 Sci-fi author who influenced many early polyamorists
2 Your sib's kid
3 Dwindle away
4 A solo act
5 Cause a Malliard reaction
6 What 7 Down might call other folks
7 A gathering of ten Jews for ceremonial purposes
8 __-a-trois
11 You're so funny!
13 A stick for striking balls
15 To help raise a kid, your own or someone else's
20 One structure for a triad
21 Indian lentil stew
22 Gobsmacked
23 Tire inflation no.
26 I'm all __!
28 Up and out of that chair
30 A ballplayer wants a high one
31 What you might ask your friends to keep about your relationship
32 Something outsiders may think poly is (but they're wrong)
33 One strategy for helping care for your family's health (abbr)
35 Another thing outsiders may think poly is (they're wrong about this one too)
36 __ marriage: a historical arrangement for sidestepping antiquated laws forbidding same-sex marriage
39 A little piece of something that was once whole
40 Chi manipulation bodywork
41 The key you hit when your boss comes in
43 That feels so good!
44 Something an alternative relationship may go out on
45 You're even funnier than 11 Down!
46 Where you can learn someone's 30 Down

Solution on page 48.

SARTRE·BEAUVOIR·ALGREN

Tara Madison Avery

25

Polyamory

BINGO

Successfully navigated jealous moment with partner	Worked with metamour to plan something for shared partner	Attended a poly munch	Dated my partner's partner or ex	Read a poly book
Attended support group/meet up with other poly folks	Played board |game with| entire polycule	Had a good time by myself	Came out to someone about being poly	Experienced poly-saturation
Differentiated a personal boundary from a relationship rule	Had a sexual experience with more than one person at a time	FREE	Made profile on dating app	Deleted profile on dating app
Loved more than one person at a time	Struck up conversation about polyamory	Communicated about communication	Listened to at least 10 episodes from a poly podcast	Found a poly-affirmative therapist
Helped a partner through a break-up	Spent one-on-one time with metamour	Experienced compersion	Argued about the best poly book or podcast	Raised a child with more than one partner

Stephanie M. Sullivan and Carrie Metz-Caporusso

Maze text (pitfalls and hazards):
- Partner works weekends!
- Both partners must be available for triad night!
- Partner with child needs babysitter for date night!
- Polycule pandemonium!
- Asexual partner: no stay over nights!
- Who has cat allergies?

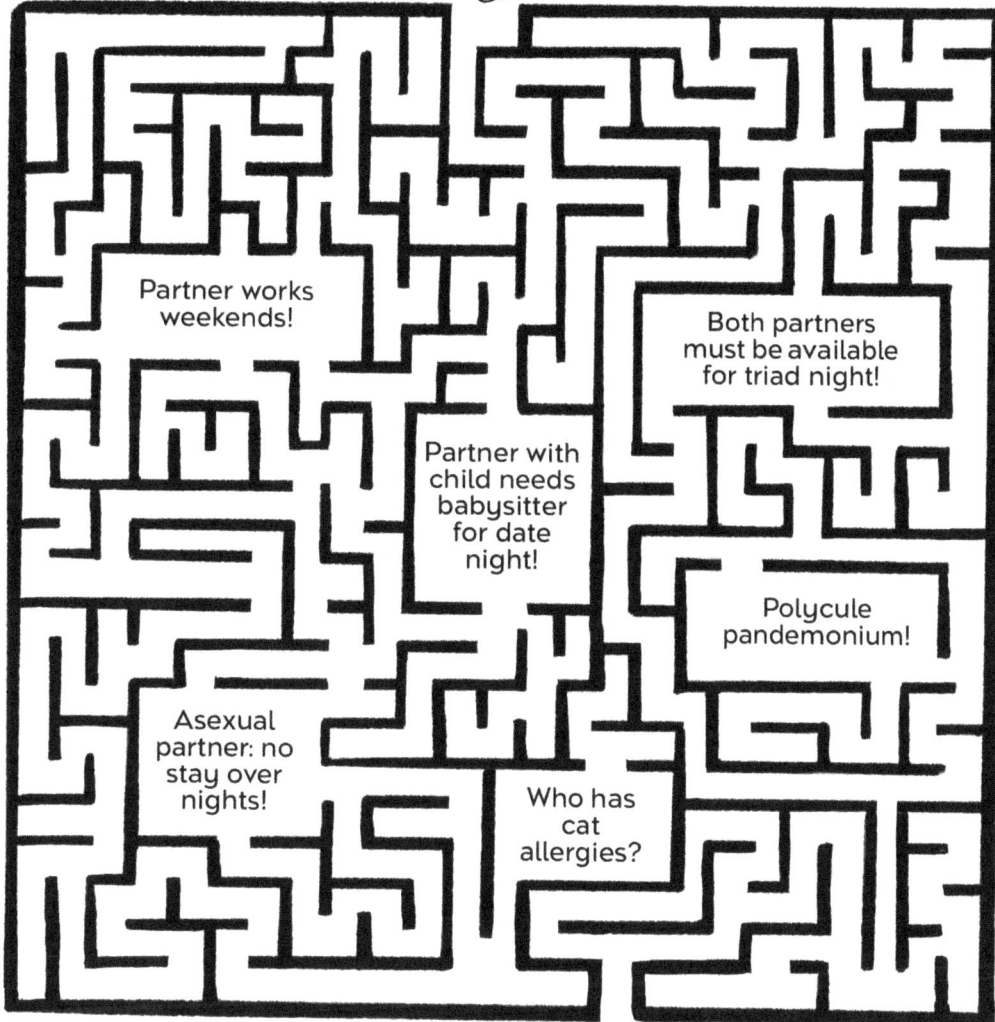

POLY SCHEDULING
MAZE PITFALLS
AND HAZARDS

Jon Macy

How to Draw a Polycule

A polycule is a group of people who are connected by their romantic relationships. This will often include partners/paramours, comets, metamours, and even partners of metamours. One way to illustrate and keep track of a connected group of romantic relationships is to draw or diagram it. While there is no one standard way of drawing a polycule, there are some common elements and practices in how they are usually represented in a diagram. Also, a single polycule can be drawn in any number of ways with a given set of symbols and guidelines. So don't be afraid you'll do it "wrong"! Jump in, sketch out your relationships, and have fun!

Getting Started:

There are two basic things that we represent in a polycule diagram: people and the relationships among them. For our purposes we will use squares labeled with names to represent people and different kinds of lines drawn between these squares to represent different kinds of relationships. In your own drawings you can add symbols or elements to represent things about your partners and relationships that are of special importance to you.

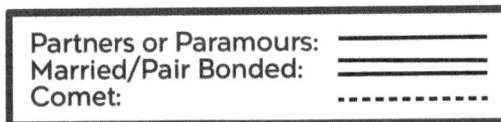

```
Partners or Paramours:   ══════════
Married/Pair Bonded:     ══════════
Comet:                   -----------
```

[Note: Our example and exercises for drawing polycules may include details such as the gender identity and sexual orientation of certain partners. These have been added for color and flavor. We have not supplied any symbols to represent these sorts of details, so please don't feel that it's necessary to include them in your drawings. However, if you would like to add them, please do and enjoy!]

Example: Matt, a cisgender bisexual man, is married to Teagan, a pansexual non-binary individual. Matt is also dating Stacy, a transgender woman. Teagan is dating Quinn and Celeste, a lesbian cisgender couple. Draw this polycule with the information given.

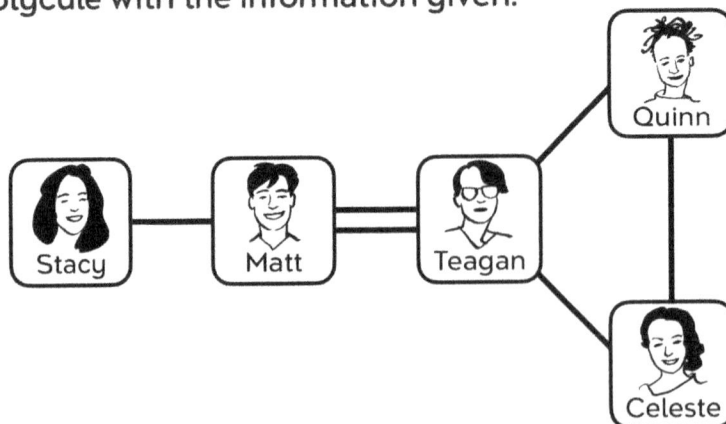

Stephanie M. Sullivan and Tara Madison Avery

Jaclyn is a straight, cisgender woman who has been practicing solo polyamory. Her partners include Jax, a trans man, Frederick, a cisgender man , and Mike, a cisgender man. Jax identifies as straight and monogamous and does not have any other partners. Frederick identifies as straight and solo poly and has one other partner, Samantha. Mike identifies as bisexual and polyamorous but currently is not seeing any other partners. Draw this polycule with the information given.

Jeremiah and Jennifer have a strong, secure attachment bond between them. One could say they are pair bonded. They recently decided to open their relationship. Jeremiah has been dating Ben, and Jennifer and Ben are dating as well. Jeremiah, Jennifer, and Ben have formed a triad. Alejandro, Ben's long-term nesting partner, has no other partners. Jennifer has also been dating Jason, who lives out of town and visits every month or so . Draw this polycule with the information given.

Are you polyamorous? Draw your own polycule!

Tara Madison Avery

"LOVING THE HECK OUTTA YOURSELF!" COLORING PAGE & SOLO ACTIVITY

Solo Activity: To get in touch with how you can give yourself love in this moment, try asking yourself how you want to be loved and write the answers using your non-dominant hand, in a stream of consciousness flow! Then creatively explore how you might be able to give yourself love and appreciation here in this room, RIGHT NOW!

Tikva Wolf

WHAT'S THE DIFFERENCE?

A LOT OF PEOPLE DON'T KNOW THAT THEY AND THEIR PARTNERS ARE ACTUALLY SEPARATE ENTITIES, WHICH BLURS THE LINE BETWEEN MAKING **RULES** FOR OTHERS, AND PERSONAL **BOUNDARIES**

Tikva Wolf

MINI POLYCULE ORBIT!

GROUP CONNECTION GAME
ADAPTED FROM THE CARD GAME BY KIMCHI CUDDLES

POLYCULE ORBIT IS A CREATIVE COMMUNICATION TOOL. THIS MINI VERSION FOCUSES ON PLAYFUL GROUP CONNECTION.

HOW TO PLAY

WITH HOWEVER MANY PEOPLE CAN FIT IN THE ROOM / VIDEO CALL, TAKE TURNS ROLLING A D4 & D12 TO PAIR CONNECTION MATCH-UPS AND USE THE CORRESPONDING TABLES TO CREATIVELY INTERACT AS LONG AS IT'S FUN.

D4 - CONNECTION TABLE

1 - MAKE A REQUEST (TO AN INDIVIDUAL OR THE WHOLE GROUP)
2 - EXPRESS AN EMOTION, THOUGHT, OR BODY SENSATION
3 - OFFER SOMEONE SOMETHING (LOVE, COMPLIMENT, ETC)
4 - EVERYONE SHARE A SYNCHRONIZED MOMENT....

D12 - CONNECTION TABLE

1 - THROUGH MOVEMENT (DANCING, FLAILING, ETC)
2 - AS AN ANIMAL VERSION OF YOURSELF
3 - THROUGH RANDOM CHAOS (TRADE SEATS, TRADE OUTFITS, ETC)
4 - SPEAKING AS YOUR INNER CHILD
5 - USING ONLY YOUR ELBOWS OR KNEES
6 - USING ONLY YOUR EYES
7 - THROUGH ROLEPLAY (MADE UP CHARACTER)
8 - USING NON-VERBAL SOUNDS AND/OR MUSIC
9 - IN THE FORM OF GRATITUDE
10 - TAPPING INTO THE JOY OR RAGE OF YOUR ANCESTORS
11 - INVOLVING SOMETHING YOU THINK ABOUT A LOT
12 - USING RANDOM OBJECTS IN THE ROOM

Relationship Comics and Card Games 🌀 tikva wolf.com

Tikva Wolf

Navigating Relationship Decisions in Polyamory: An Example

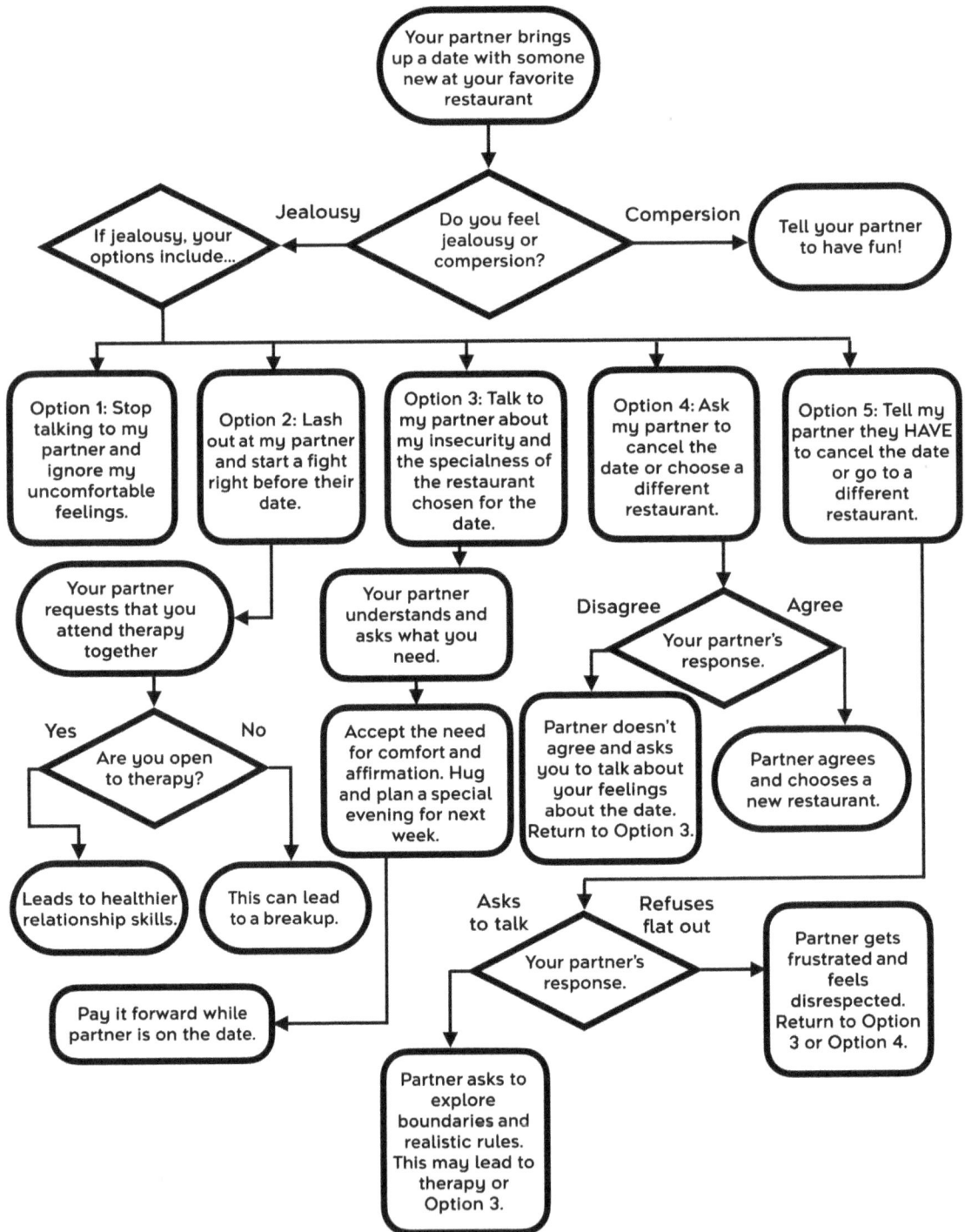

Your partner brings up a date with somone new at your favorite restaurant

↓

Do you feel jealousy or compersion?

Jealousy → If jealousy, your options include...

Compersion → Tell your partner to have fun!

Option 1: Stop talking to my partner and ignore my uncomfortable feelings.

Option 2: Lash out at my partner and start a fight right before their date.

Option 3: Talk to my partner about my insecurity and the specialness of the restaurant chosen for the date.

Option 4: Ask my partner to cancel the date or choose a different restaurant.

Option 5: Tell my partner they HAVE to cancel the date or go to a different restaurant.

Your partner requests that you attend therapy together

Are you open to therapy?
- **Yes** → Leads to healthier relationship skills.
- **No** → This can lead to a breakup.

Your partner understands and asks what you need.

Accept the need for comfort and affirmation. Hug and plan a special evening for next week.

Pay it forward while partner is on the date.

Your partner's response.
- **Disagree** → Partner doesn't agree and asks you to talk about your feelings about the date. Return to Option 3.
- **Agree** → Partner agrees and chooses a new restaurant.

Your partner's response.
- **Asks to talk** → Partner asks to explore boundaries and realistic rules. This may lead to therapy or Option 3.
- **Refuses flat out** → Partner gets frustrated and feels disrespected. Return to Option 3 or Option 4.

Kathleen McMahon

Mix Tapes of Love

Use this activity to create short playlist for your partners! Each cassette has a space for you and your partners names, Label them accordingly and merge your love into a playlist of 16 songs that describe your partnership!

"B" SIDE

B:

A

A:

Iggy "Eggs" Morris

Leah Spears

Janet W. Hardy

Nesting Partners

Power Exchange Dynamic

Queer Platonic Relationship

Leah Spears

The Comanche

Ross Vegas

Kwai Fa

Pouty and Polly

SHOULDN'T YOU TELL PAUL ABOUT US?

NAH, IT'S OKAY. WE'RE POLY...

POUTY DOESN'T INFORM HIS POLYCULE ABOUT HIS NEW SEXUAL PARTNERS.

I'VE STARTED SEEING KIM. SHE'S MARRIED, USES SAFER SEX PRACTICES, AND IS NEW TO POLY.

POLLY UPDATES HER WHOLE POLYCULE ON HER SEXUAL ACTIVITY AND HEALTH.

WOULD YOU LIKE A FREE HIV TEST?

NAH, MAN. I THINK ALL MY PARTNERS ARE CLEAN...

POUTY DOESN'T SEE THE NEED FOR REGULAR STI TESTING.

I TESTED LAST MONTH. STILL ALL NEGATIVE.

I JUST SCHEDULED MY ANNUAL TESTS.

POLLY COORDINATES ANNUAL STI TESTING WITH HER WHOLE POLYCULE.

Tara Madison Avery

41

Kwai Fa

HISTORICAL INFO

Editors note.

Every group, person, or relationship depicted in this book has a unique story. Not all of the people depicted were ethical in their relationships, and some may have been harmful to others. The editors chose to include these histories in order to attempt to encapsulate many different stories and experiences in non-monogamy. However, their inclusion does not mean that the editors or contributors agree with non-ethical or non-consensual relationships. By contrast, we believe that information about what doesn't work, and what is harmful, is just as important as knowing what does work and what is not harmful, so as not to continue to make these kinds of mistakes.

Bloomsbury Group

The Bloomsbury Group was a loosely knit collection of writers, thinkers, and artists based in early 20th Century England. The name of the group is derived from the fashionable Bloomsbury district in London's West End. The shifting roster of members included literary, aesthetic, and intellectual figures such as Vanessa Bell, Clive Bell, Lytton Strachey, Virginia Woolf, Leonard Woolf, Roger Fry, Duncan Grant, Maynard Keynes, and Vita Sackville-West. Members of the group, sometimes called "Bloomsberries", were partners and lovers in various interconnected relationships, with both same-sex and different-sex pairings throughout the years. Vanessa Bell and Duncan Grant moved to a farmhouse in Sussex and had a child together. Their sexual relationship appears to have been brief, though their care for one another was long-lasting. The farmhouse was considered a "living artwork" and an "experiment in living" as lovers came and went through the years. Clive Bell had his own room and Roger Fry designed a studio space there.

Kerista Community

The Kerista Commune flourished in the San Francisco area from 1971 to 1991. However, the initial idea for this community started in the 1950s with its founder, John Presmont (Brother Jud), who made many attempts to find a meaningful religious and communal lifestyle before founding the Kerista Commune. Kerista was an attempt to found a "utopian" and intentional community. Among its achievements, Kerista is credited with coining the terms "compersion" (the opposite of jealousy; positive feelings about your partner's other intimacies) and "polyfidelity" (fidelitous to many partners). Membership in the commune fluctuated throughout the years, and at its peak it had about 30 members. Members of the Kerista Commune shared income and had multiple income ventures. In addition, they attempted to have "non-preferential" relationships with one another and were on a rotational sleeping schedule with members of the other sex. Kerista was criticized for not being egalitarian and being ultimately destructive by both outsiders and ex-Keristans.

Lavender Hill

Lavender Hill was a gay and lesbian commune started in 1973 outside of Ithica, New York. It was considered an experiment in collaboration, gender exploration, and social and political integration between young gay and lesbian individuals after Stonewall. Lavender Hill remained together for about ten years until the breakup of one gay couple that was at the center of the group. Another member also fell victim to AIDS in the 1980s, and his death heralded the end of the Lavender Hill commune.

William Mouton Marston, Elizabeth Marston, and Olive Byrne

William Marston was an American psychologist born May 9, 1893 in Massachusetts. He earned his PhD in Psychology in 1921 from Harvard University. From there, he taught at multiple universities and later developed the systolic blood pressure test, which was used as a component in developing the polygraph. Marston was also the creator of the popular comic book character, Wonder Woman. There has been speculation as to the inspiration of the Wonder Woman character, and whether she was based off of his wife, Elizabeth Holloway Marston, and his partner, Olive Byrne (who was also Margaret Sanger's niece). William, Elizabeth, and Olive lived together for many years, and William had two children with each Elizabeth (a son and a daughter) and Olive (two sons). Elizabeth worked outside of the home as a lawyer while Olive stayed at home and took care of all four children. Instead of a wedding ring, Olive wore a pair of bracelets, which were a possible inspiration for Wonder Woman's Bracelets of Submission. Marjorie Wilkes Huntley also occasionally lived with the family when she was in town. Some sources refer to her as an "aunt" to the children, and report that she also engaged in bondage with the adults of the family. On May 2, 1947, William Mouton Marston passed away, just before his 54th birthday, due to cancer. After his death, Elizabeth and Olive continued to live together until Olive's death in 1990. They had lived together for 64 years.

Oneida Community

The Oneida Community was founded in 1848 near Oneida, New York. They were a communal religious society that believed Jesus had already returned, allowing humans to live free of sin in this world, not just in Heaven. With this, the community believed in "free love" (a term which the founder, John Humphrey Noyes, is credited with coining), and complex marriage, such that any member was free to have sex with any other member who consented. Exclusive relationships were frowned upon.

Noyes believed that sexual intercourse had two distinct purposes: procreation and the expression of love. In order to avoid unwanted pregnancies, the members of the Oneida Community practiced what Noyes called "male continence" - the avoidance of ejaculation. Older women were paired as sexual mentors with male adolescents to "train" them on male continence, and younger women were paired with older, more experienced men. Children were raised communally, and many children were born based on eugenic "pairings" chosen by Noyes. However, women were also afforded more freedoms in the community than they had in broader society at that time, including playing an active role in shaping commune policies.

The Oneida Community began to manufacture bags, hats, garden furniture, and eventually, silverware, and established the manufacturing firm Oneida Limited. The community disbanded in 1881, but the silverware company still exists today.

Cadmus-French-French (PaJaMa)

Paul Cadmus, Jared French, and Margaret French were visual artists and polyamorous partners known collectively to friends and artists' circles as PaJaMa. They met in New York City at the Art Students League. Paul and Jared became lovers, and Jared married Margaret Hoening in 1937. The triad remained together as partners and created art together for 20 years, in particular their photographic work set against the beaches of New England and New York. Their pioneering homoerotic artwork was only shared amongst themselves and their friends until its reappraisal in the 1980s.

Simone de Beauvoir and Jean-Paul Sartre

Simone de Beauvoir was a French writer, existentialist philosopher, feminist, and social theorist born January 9, 1908. She is best known for her feminist treatise, The Second Sex, as well as her novels such as The

Mandarins and She Came to Stay. Her novel She Came to Stay has been described as a fictionalization of her open relationship with Jean-Paul Sartre and another woman he was dating, or possibly a composite of multiple women.

Jean-Paul Sartre was a French writer, existentialist philosopher, political activist, and literary critic born June 21, 1905. He is best known for his contributions to existentialist philosophy and phenomenology, including his principal philosophical work, Being and Nothingness. He was awarded the Nobel Prize for Literature in 1964, and attempted to decline the award, stating that he did not want to be "transformed" by this type of award and was uninterested in participating in an East-West cultural struggle by accepting a Western award.

Simone de Beauvoir and Jean-Paul Sartre never married or lived together; however, they would meet daily to talk, write, edit, and share details of their other relationships. They were together as partners for over 50 years, and their only requirement in their relationship was to be honest and transparent with one another. However, they may not have felt this way about the other partners they had, especially Sartre, who would often pursue much younger women for short relationships without informing them about his other paramours. De Beauvoir appears to have had longer-term and more intimate relationships, including with American author Nelson Algren, most famous for his novel The Man with the Golden Arm. The relationship between the two lasted nearly two years, but ended acrimoniously, with Algren denigrating the amorous exploits of both Beauvoir and Sarte in public forums including Playboy Magazine. However, de Beauvoir also engaged in some exploitative relationships with much younger women, including a student, whom she temporarily lost her teaching license over. Sartre and de Beauvoir were buried together in Paris.

Bonobos

Of all primates, bonobos and chimpanzees are the closest genetic relatives to humans. It has been argued that bonobos are remarkably like humans when it comes to their sexuality and relationships. For example, chimps and other primates use sexuality primarily for reproduction. Bonobos, on the other hand, are highly sexual creatures and utilize sex for social purposes - such as reducing tension, bonding, conflict resolution, and entertainment - much as humans do. Bonobos and humans also often gaze into one another's eyes and kiss deeply before copulation, whereas chimps do neither. In addition, bonobos and humans both enjoy many different positions when copulating, and it is common to see same-sex bonobos engaging in sexual activity. Chimps, on the other hand, prefer the rear-entry copulatory position almost exclusively, and it is rare to see same-sex sexual activity between chimps. Bonobos also experience multiple sexual partners, and do not have monogamous mating or pair bonds. Female bonobos will often mate with multiple males in quick succession. The argument for humans being "naturally" monogamous or non-monogamous continues to this day, and research on bonobo sexuality and mating patterns have been a large part of the debate.

Kevin Patterson

Kevin Patterson is an author and educator who is an active member of the Philadelphia polyamory community. He has been practicing ethical nonmonogamy since 2002. In 2015, Patterson started Poly Role Models, in which people had the chance to describe their polyamorous experiences in an interview context. Poly Role Models strives to be inclusive of diverse voices within the polyamorous community. Patterson, to continue increasing representation of the polyamorous community, then began doing speaking engagements about the intersection of race and polyamory. This work led him to write Love's Not Colorblind: Race and Representation in Polyamorous and Other Alternative Communities. He has also written, with co-author Alana Phelan, a science fiction series titled For Hire, which centers characters of color and of other marginalized communities.

The Comanche Tribe

The Comanche tribe practiced polygamy for several centuries before the imposition of United States law in Oklahoma Territory. As members of a warrior tribe, young Comanche men frequently perished in battle against western colonizing forces. This led to a population imbalance of two or more women for every man, and the culture adopted the practice of polygamy. Comanche men took multiple wives who looked after agriculture, children, and the home. This was a patriarchal practice with wives subordinate to their husbands, and some abusive practices on the part of men toward their spouses have been documented. Wives were also not permitted to interact socially with men who were not their husbands. However, this practice was embraced by both Comanche men and women and persisted through much of the 20th century until completely phased out under U.S. law.

PUZZLE SOLUTIONS

Crossword Puzzle Solution

Word Search Solution

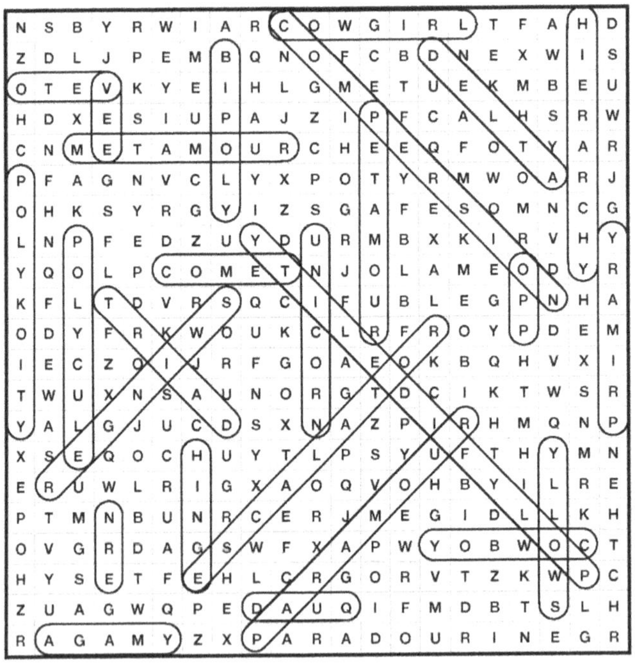

Scramble solution

IRENICEGV SGFTI	RECEIVING GIFTS
MAOLYOYPR	POLYAMORY
YHCPISAL HTUOC	PHYSICAL TOUCH
CMOSPNIOER	COMPERSION
CAST FO RCSEVIE	ACTS OF SERVICE
ESUYCORELP	POLYSECURE
ROWDS FO FAIAORINMFT	WORDS OF AFFIRMATION
LLEPUYOC	POLYCULE
QAUYTLI TEIM	QUALITY TIME
TAMMOUER	METAMOUR

Polyamory Glossary
By Stephanie M. Sullivan M.S., LMFT

Agamy: The absence of marriage or the state of being unmarried. This could also be a lack of acknowledgment of the institution of marriage or full opposition to the idea of marriage.

Ambiamory: A relationship orientation in which individuals can be comfortable and happy in either polyamorous or monogamous relationships. Ambiamorists may be open to relationship structures that fit the individuals involved in them as well as the life situations in which they find themselves.

Bipoly: Someone who identifies as both bisexual and polyamorous; many polyamorous relationships will include at least one person who is bipoly.

Cheating: Acting dishonestly in a relationship, breaking a relationship agreement, and/or having a secret sexual or emotional relationship outside of an established relationship without the consent of all parties involved.

Comet: Someone who is an occasional lover; there will often not be an expectation of an ongoing romantic or sexual relationship, but will rather come in and out of one's life intermittently.

Compersion: To feel joy or delight when one's beloved loves or is being loved by another.

Compulsory Monogamy: The social mandate that everyone must be in a monogamous relationship in order to be considered a morally upstanding adult. Compulsory monogamy is embedded in norms, institutions, and laws. See also: idealized monogamy, mononormativity.

Conscious Monogamy: Choosing to be monogamous with a partner as an agreement, with full knowledge that there are other ethical non-monogamous options and still choosing monogamy due to preference, orientation, or life circumstances.

Cowboy/Cowgirl: Someone who is ultimately monogamous and meets someone who is polyamorous, becomes romantically involved with them, and attempts to get them to become monogamous with them. Will often encourage the polyamorous person to leave their existing relationships and/or stop dating, therefore "cutting them out of the herd." Not a compliment.

Delta: Three people engaged in a sexual and/or romantic relationship with one another. See also: menage-a-trois, triad.

Handfasting: An ancient Celtic ritual in which a couples' hands are tied together to symbolize the binding of two lives.

Hierarchy/Hierarchical Polyamory: A relationship structure in which a person has multiple partners, but those partners are not equal in terms of interconnection, emotional intensity, and/or power within the relationship. Individuals who practice hierarchical polyamory place more importance on one relationship above other relationships, which may be known as the primary relationship. The primary may be prioritized above other relationships in regards to time commitments, vacations and holidays, going to family functions, and other important events. Other partners may be considered secondary or tertiary. Secondary or tertiary partners may not be taken into account when big decisions are being made, and if the individual is not "out" as polyamorous, could even be kept hidden from friends and family.

Hinge: Someone who is involved with two people who are not involved with each other. Hinges are often part of vee relationships.

Idealized Monogamy: The idea that monogamy is the superior or best choice for anyone in a society, and that everyone should be monogamous, regardless of infidelity or unhappiness. See also: compulsory monogamy, mononormativity.

Menage-a-trois: An arrangement in which three people have a sexual and/or romantic relationship with one another, especially when they are living together domestically. Could also be a single sexual encounter between three people; a threesome. See also: delta, triad.

Metamour/Meta: Metamours are two people who are dating the same person, but are not actively dating each other. Metamours may not know one another, may be vague acquaintances, or may be very good friends. In some cases, metamours may even live with one another, with or without their shared partner.

Mononormativity: Refers to the dominant societal assumptions that monogamy is normal and natural. Also refers to the practices or institutions that value or privilege monogamous relationships as fundamental and natural within a society. See also: compulsory monogamy, idealized monogamy.

New Relationship Energy (NRE): A state of mind experienced at the beginning of sexual and romantic relationships, typically involving heightened emotional and sexual feelings and excitement.

Non-Hierarchy/Non-Hierarchical Polyamory: A relationship structure in which individuals within the relationship believe that one partner does not hold importance over another, and each relationship is important in its own way. This does not necessarily mean that time is split equally between two or more partners, nor does it mean that all the partners live together. It does mean that every partner is considered when making big decisions.

Nuclear Family: A family group consisting of two parents and their child(ren). It is differentiated from a single-parent family, a larger extended family, or a family with more than two parents.

Old Relationship Energy (ORE): The dynamic of a long-standing established romantic or sexual relationship, in which one feels a strong level of comfort and contentment in their relationship.

One Penis Policy (OPP): An agreement between a typically heterosexual-appearing couple in which they agree that the woman can have sexual and/or romantic relationships with other women but not with other men. The man, however, can have relationships with other women. Often viewed as unequal and problematic, OPPs can be based in sexism, biphobia and transphobia, and are often adopted as a result of jealousy or insecurity. There may be reasons OPPs are freely chosen and accepted by all involved - for example, when a bisexual woman in a heterosexual-appearing monogamous relationship is interested in connecting with another woman in a sexual and/or romantic relationship.

Open Relationship: A relationship in which one or more parties have consent to be romantically and/or sexually involved with someone outside of their relationship. This is as opposed to a "closed," or exclusive relationship. Open relationships are non-monogamous in at least one way. Can also be considered an umbrella term for polyamory, swinging, monogamish, or any other relationship style that is not monogamous.

Pair Bonding: A behavioral and/or physiological bond between two animals or people. Often considered a "mated pair," pair bonds can be lifelong and can lead to the production and rearing of offspring.

Paramour: A gender-neutral term to refer to one's lover or partner.

Petamour: A term to refer to a pet that is in one's life due to their polyamorous connections; this may refer to a metamour's pet or a partner's pet.

Polyamory/Polyam: Polyamory is a relationship style or orientation centered on the belief that it is possible to love more than one person romantically. Polyamorous relationships often involve having more than one romantic relationship simultaneously, with full knowledge and consent of all the partners involved.

Polycule: A group of people who are connected by their romantic relationships. This will often include partners/paramours, comets, metamours, and even partners of metamours.

Polyfidelity: A relationship structure in which all members are partners and agree to restrict sexual or romantic activity only to current partners in the group. Fidelitous polyamory.

Polygamy: The practice of marrying multiple spouses.

Polysaturated: When one feels as though they have as many relationships as they can handle in their current life; when they do not have the time or emotional energy to add another partner.

Quad: A quad is made up of four partners who are intimately connected in some way, whether romantically or sexually. A quad can be formed in a multitude of ways, such as a triad adding another partner. Quads can also be formed when two couples connect and begin dating, forming the quad.

Relationship Anarchy: A relationship style or orientation in which individuals believe that all interpersonal relationships are equally important. A relationship anarchist might have multiple romantic relationships simultaneously, but may also avoid making special distinctions between relationships that are romantic, sexual, platonic, or familial. They often avoid putting relationships into categories or having expectations in their relationships. Instead, they allow their relationships to take any form and have any level of commitment that the participants decide to have.

Relationship Escalator: The default set of societal expectations for intimate relationships. Partners follow a progressive set of steps (e.g., dating, having sex, moving in together) with visible markers toward a clear goal (e.g., marriage, having children).The Escalator is the standard by which most people in Western societies gauge whether a developing intimate relationship is significant, healthy, committed, or worth continuing.

Solo/SoPo/Solo Polyamory: A relationship structure in which the individual does not have any desire to be considered part of a "coupled" relationship and may consider themself to be their own primary relationship. Although solo polyamorists usually do not choose to live with their partner(s), this does not mean that they do not have one or more deeply committed and intimate relationships.

Swinger/Swinging: A relationship style or orientation in which, generally, there is an established couple and agreements in which sexual relations occur outside of this couple, usually where they are swapping partners with another couple or engaging in group sex. Swingers tend to refrain from romantic attachments outside of their already-established relationship(s).

Swolly: A person who identifies as both a swinger and as polyamorous; someone who has multiple simultaneous relationships and engages in recreational sex in a swinging context.

Triad: A triad is made up of three partners in which all three partners are romantically and/or sexually involved with each other. See also: delta, menage-a-trois.

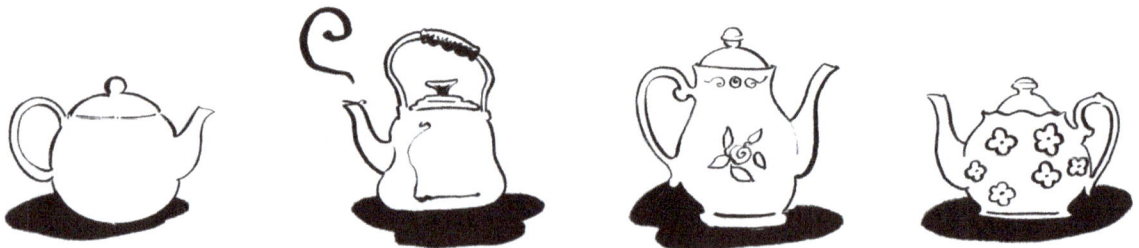

Unicorn: Usually defined as a beautiful polyamorous bisexual woman who may want to date or have sex with both partners in a heterosexual-appearing relationship. Considered to be rare and hard to find, hence the term "unicorn."

Unicorn Hunters: Typically a heterosexual-appearing couple looking for a woman to join their relationship as it is and either date or have casual sex with them both. Often, this couple is deciding how they want the triadic relationship to be before they have even met the woman, or "unicorn." They are often looking for a relationship already having highly specific expectations for their desired third partner.

Vee: A vee relationship is made up of three partners and gets its name from the letter "V," in which one person acts as the "hinge" or "pivot" partner dating two people. The other two people are not romantically or sexually involved with each other and are metamours rather than partners.

Veto: Having a veto, or veto power, in a relationship generally occurs in relationships in which there is an already-established primary or hierarchical relationship. One, both, or all partners will have the option to forbid another partner from dating a specific person or continuing a specific relationship. This creates a stronger hierarchy in the relationship without allowing the third partner (the one being vetoed) to make a choice about their own relationship.

We supply the queer history.
You supply the color.

The LGBTQ+ Historical Coloring Book Series.
Only from Stacked Deck Press.

Real historical
figures drawn
by today's most
talented queer
cartoonists and
illustrators

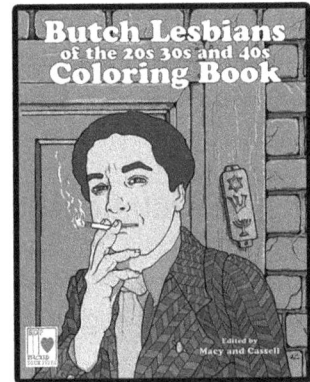

The Queer Heroes
Coloring Book
By Jon Macy and
Tara Madison Avery

The Butch Lesbians of the '20s,
'30s, and '40s Coloring Book
By Jon Macy and Avery Cassell

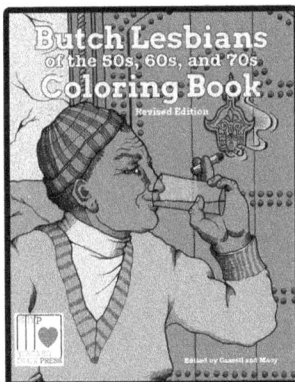

Each book includes
biographical
details of the
subjects depicted

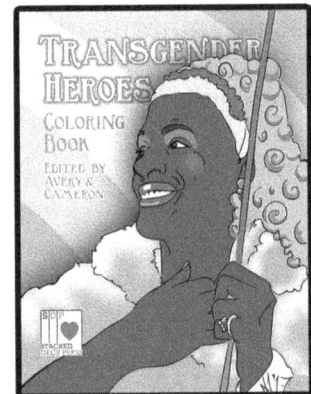

The Butch Lesbians of the '50s,
'60s, and '70s Coloring Book
By Avery Cassell and Jon Macy

The Transgender Heroes
Coloring Book
By Tara Madison Avery
and Gillian Cameron

Find these and more at
stackeddeckpress.com!
Also available on Amazon!

SDP
STACKED
DECK PRESS

www.ingramcontent.com/pod-product-compliance
Lightning Source LLC
Chambersburg PA
CBHW081723270326
41933CB00017B/3277